Strange Unexplained True Mysteries

- Volume 1

Frank Baker

Contents

Introduction

The world holds many strange mysteries and strange incidents occur every day.

In this book there are a collection of weird and eerie tales of the unexplained. From headless ghosts to small green aliens on a moor. From strange phone calls from the dead to human blood leaking from a ceiling during a dinner party. These mysteries will hopefully fascinate as well as scare.

I hope you enjoy this carefully selected spooky compilation of chilling and bizarre unexplained mysteries - Strange Unexplained True Mysteries - Volume 1.

Calvados Chateau

In 1875 a number of mysterious incidents happened at the Château des Noyers du Tourneur in the Calvados village of Le Tourneur in Normandy, France. A diarist known as X who was resident in the Castle kept an account of the macabre disturbances. The diarist was Ferdinand de Manville; but he wanted his identify kept secret and gave is name as X in his diary.

One evening the residents in the castle were in bed when strange noises started to emanate from the castle walls. The mysterious noises included weeping and a tapping sound on the walls. The people resident in the house were X, his wife and son, his son's tutor Emile, a coachman and three servants. The ghostly noises went on for several days.

X thought that someone was making the noises and pretending to be the supernatural forces. He decided to set a trap. He placed very thin strings on thread in the doorways in the entrances to the castle. If the threads were broken, then that would prove someone was making the noises and pretending to be the ghosts. But after another night of horror and various strange occurrences the threads were found to be untouched.

X then decided to start keeping a diary of the disturbances; the first entry was on the 13th October 1875. On that night his son's tutor experienced some strange phenomenon. A candle was lifted from the mantle piece. Taps were heard on the wall. X went to the room and found that the armchair had also moved. Emile and X searched the castle for the next several days to try and find what was behind the strange noises emanating from the castle walls.

A few weeks later X recorded in his diary that the noises were continuing with huge "blows that rocked the whole castle".

The noises started to get louder and louder. On the evening of November 10th X wrote about a torturous night. After 1 am shrieks were heard: a woman's scream appealing for help. Furniture was moved, bibles were torn up, X's wife went to close a door, but her hand was knocked by an unseen force forcing her to drop the key. Her hand was bruised for 2 days. She also heard a constant hammering on the door all night. The noises and the general reign of terror continued.

On January 6th 1976 there was a terrifying set of horrific incidents at the castle. x wrote it sounded as if demons were driving herds of wild cattle through the room". Demonic laughter was heard.

On January 15th a priest - The Rev. Fr. H.L. - was brought in in an attempt to exorcise the supernatural forces at the castle. The priest placed all the religious artifacts in the castle in the room where the noises were heard. This worked and the grisly noises came to an end.

There was a strange epilogue to the tale. One morning at the castle the religious artifacts disappeared. Later when X's wife sat writing at a desk the artifacts were dropped on the floor one by one in front of her. This strange incident was followed by more strange noises, before silence finally fell upon the Chateau.

The family sold the house in 1877 tired of the supernatural incidents. The chateau was destroyed in a strange fire in 1984. The chateau had been built on the site of a former medieval castle that had a reputation for strange activities involving ghosts and even werewolves.

Hannah Beswick

Hannah Beswick was a rich landowner who owned land near Manchester in England. In 1745 Scotchman Bonnie Prince Charlie invaded England and was advancing southwards. Beswick was scared that the marauding Scotch would rob her. She decided to hide her money and valuables.

One of Beswick's relatives had be thought to be dead after falling ill. Her brother John showed signs of life in his coffin while being visited by relatives. His eyelids were seen to flicker. John recovered a few days later. This gave Bewsick a morbid fear of being buried alive.

In 1768 Beswick passed away. She died having not told anyone where her valuables were stored. As she did not want to be buried she requested that after death her body be kept above ground.

Another bizarre request was that every two years her body should be placed in her old house for seven days. Her body was mummified - covered in bandages with her face showing. Hannah's mummified body was kept at Sale Priory, the house of doctor Charles White who was charged with carrying out Hannah's wishes.

After Dr White's death the body was moved to the Natural History Society Museum in Manchester and the body made a popular exhibit. Beswick's mummified body was displayed next to am Egyptian and Peruvian mummy. The body was known as the Manchester Mummy and The Mummy of Birchin Tower.

In 1868, 100 years after Hannah Beswick's death, the museum's authorities decided the body should finally have a proper burial. Her body was interred at Harpurhey Cemetery in Manchester.

After her death Hannah had been sighted at her old house at Birchin Bower. She was dressed in a black silk gown and white lace cap. She often walked between an old barn and a pond looking worried; it was even reported that the barn seemed to glow during her visitations.

Hannah's old house was eventually turned into

multiple dwellings for mill workers. These new residents often saw the ghost of Hannah. Hannah often stared at a flagstone on the floor in a certain room. The occupant of the room decided to look under the flagstone and found some gold. After this discovery of some of Hannah's fortune she was spotted looking angry with "blue light emanating from her eyes".

She continued to haunt the barn, and stranger noises were often heard there. It is thought that Hannah was trying to protect her fortune buried near the barn.

The house was eventually demolished and Farranti an electronics company built a factory on the site. The hauntings continued with Hannah seen inside the factory.

The Phantom Gardener

In November 1945 young Peter Turner and a group of his friends were playing in some half demolished houses in Leeds in Yorkshire, England. The houses made a great playground for the children.

Peter was playing on the top floor of a house which had had its floorboards removed. He looked out of the window and was surprised to see any rubble or broken glass in the garden of the house. Instead there was an old man tending a garden.

The garden was in full bloom. Peter and his friends were scared of being caught in the house. They knew their parents would not want them playing in the derelict buildings as they were dangerous. They decided to leave.

The following day Peter realised how strange his encounter had been. Why had the man been tending a garden in full bloom in November in the north of England? He returned to the spot where he had seen the garden. This time there was no man and no garden. Just rubble.

Eleven years later Peter was planning his wedding in Leeds. Peter and his wife to be Pamela had obtained a top floor flat in a Georgian house in the city. The house had previously been a nursery.

One evening Peter and two friends were redecorating the flat. Two of them went out to get fish and chips for dinner. When they returned they found the other person outside the flat scared to go in. He had felt a strange presence in the flat and had heard a series of strange noises.

Peter duly got married and moved into the flat with Pamela. But strange occurrences soon started to happen. Cupboard doors opened and footsteps were heard. Pamela often felt like there was someone behind her in the kitchen. One evening the couple were asleep in bed when they were woken by the settee being dragged around the living room. When they checked the living room the settee was in its usual spot. The sounds continued for several nights. In the morning everything was always in place. The neighbours in the flat below began to complain about the noises, saying they "should not be moving furniture late at night."

The Turners met an old lady who had been born in the building. She said there was a room in the house which was haunted by a Victorian woman. The woman would search the nursery for her two children who had died there.

The Turners decided to find somewhere else to live.

The Walsingham Bones

An American farmer named Walsingham bought a new home in Oakville Georgia near the Savannah River.

He was looking around his home when he made a rather grisly discovery: an old skeleton. He decided to dispose of the skeleton by throwing it into a lime kiln.

After the skeleton was disposed of a number of strange incidents started to occur in the home. Doors slammed, bells tolled, chairs were upturned. Walsingham was not a believer in the supernatural and blamed his neighbours. He believed they were playing pranks on him.

The year was 1891, and mysterious events continued to happen in the Walsingham house. New events occurred which Walsingham could not blame on his neighbours and he could not find a logical answer. Strange laughter was heard in the house. Walsingham's daughter saw a hand on her shoulder; the hand was not attached to any body. Walsingham saw footprints appear next to him when he walked outside.

The Walsinghams held a dinner party. This was marred by a selection of strange events. Red liquid dripped from the ceiling, staining the white table cloth. Extremely odd noises and groans were heard from the room above the dining room. The men went up to investigate the room above. They found nothing, even after taking up the floorboards. The liquid was later identified as human blood. The Walsinghams decided to sell the house.

The house fell into disrepair as no one wanted to live there. The place was said to have a strange, gloomy atmosphere.

It is said that several months after the Walsinghams left the house a man named Horace Gunn bet a friend that he could spend a night alone in the house. He reported that he could not get a fire to light. He heard laughter, screams and sounds of people running up and down the stairs. One terrifying incident was a human head floating around the room. Gunn then said:

"Then it vanished, but there broke out in the room a loud and awe-inspiring wail as of several souls in anguish. I thought then that I could see indistinct shapes flitting about, and, mustering up all my courage, I attempted to pass them and gain the door. But just as I reached it, I felt my ankle seized in a firm grasp; I was thrown down and felt fingers grasping at my throat..."

He was found unconscious on the floor the next morning.

The house was eventually demolished. Bones were found under the house. It was theorised that they may be those of murder victims. Perhaps the skeleton Walsingham through into the kiln was the skeleton of one of the ghosts haunting the house.

Messages From The Dead

In 1971 Mr C.E. and Mrs Bonnie MacConnell were telephoned at their Tuscon, Arizona home by their friend Enid Johlson. The elderly Mrs Johlson had been moved to a different nursing home and had subsequently lost touch with the MacConnells. The MacConnells were pleased to hear from Mrs Johlson who had got in touch again after a while.

Mrs MacConnell promised to pay Mrs Johlson a visit and take her some of Enid's favourite brandy.

Enid said she was not a brandy drinker now and said "I won't need it now". Enid stated that her health had been better.

A week later Mrs MacConnell called Enid's nursing home to chat to Enid and arrange a visit. The receptionist at the home had some bad news. Enid had died the previous Sunday - hours before the first phone call to Mrs MacConnell.

The Rev. Carl Hewitt was a psychic medium. In the 1970s Rev Carl Hewitt had hired a secretary to take care of his appointments as he was rather busy.

One afternoon his secretary received a very eerie call. The voice - who was called Robert - had asked to make an appointment for a physic reading with the Rev. Hewitt. Apparently the voice "did not sound human".

The following day Hewitt's secretary rang Robert to confirm the appointment for the reading. Robert was angry and said he had never made an appointment and did not believe in psychic mediums. But eventually he agreed to come to the appointment.

The next day he attended the reading and spoke to the Rev Hewitt. The Rev Hewitt became aware of a young man called Fred in the room with them. Robert was angry during the meeting, but the Reverend got him to calm down. Then Fred asked The Rev Hewitt to pass on a message. Fred was Robert's son, and he said he had not committed suicide as Robert thought.

The telephone rang in the Indianapolis home of Viola Tollen It had just got dark in the evening. She had a strange conversation with a small child. Violet thought she recognised the voice. The voice said:

"They said i could telephone you, and I have".

Violet asked who the caller was. "I know your voice" she said. The child responded "you know me - I'm ruby".Ruby Stone had been a neighbour of Mrs Tollen. They had been friends.

Unfortunately Ruby had died aged only 7. Violet had received a phone call from the dead.

In 1988 on September horror author Dean Koontz was working on a book when the telephone rang. It was a woman. The voice said: "Please be careful". The woman repeated the phrase three more times. Koontz asked her who she was but she did not respond. Soon the line was cut off.

Koontz was confused as to who the caller could be. It was difficult to make a prank call to him as his number was unlisted. He thought the voice sounded similar to his dead mother.

A few days later Koontz visited his father who lived in a retirement home. His father suffered from dementia. He had a strange experience with

his father who tried to cut him with a fishing knife.
Koontz managed to take the knife off his father.
But when the police arrived they thought Koontz
was attacking his father and very nearly shot him.
Koontz just managed to tell them what was really
happening.

Koontz realised the phone call was warning him
that this incident with hid father was going to
occur.

The Dentist Surgery Voices

Dentist Dr Karl Bachseitz had a surgery in the
German town of Neutraubling. He was assisted in
the surgery by 17 year old Claudia Jundenmann.

In 1982 a female patient at the surgery used the
spittoon. A voice from the spittoon said "shut your
mouth". The following week a male patient
thought that he heard the wash basin in the
surgery say "open your mouth stupid". Later that
week a woman patient used the toilet. The toilet
seemed to say "move your behind - I can't see a
thing".

These bizarre voices in the surgery continued for
a year driving Dr Bachseitz insane. The voice
became more frequent in his surgery interrupting
him over ten times a day. The voice had a
guttural Bavarian accent and constantly abused
the Dr and his patients. The voice even stated it

was going to attack the Doctor's wife. The voice gave itself the rather bizarre name of Chopper.

The voice seemed to like Claudia, the Doctor's assistant. It spoke nicely to her often asking how she spent her free time. The Dr had the surgery searched for electrical devices which could be behind the voices. But none were found. Spiritualists visited the surgery. A hit pop song was about the affair was redecorated.

In February 1982 Dr Bachseitz decided to call in an exorcist. The exorcist was the famous parapsychology expert Hans Bender. Bender spoke to the voice. The voice said to Bender " help - please release me". The telephone was disconnected, but still rang.

Later the case was solved. Claudia told the police it was a hoax and that an unknown man was behind the voices. Claudia said she invented the voice to get attention and relieve boredom. Claudia and the Dr and his were fined for "making false claims". The German post office also gave them a hefty fine. Claudia appeared on German television and spoke about the case.

But mystery surrounded why the Dr played such as bizarre practical joke. And could a real person really make the voices from a telephone?

Claudia changed her name to escape attention. The Dr and his wife were so stressed they had to check themselves into a mental institution.

The Ghostly Chess Player

Maurice Tillet was an extremely tall wrestler. Unconventional looking he was highly cultured and intelligent. He spoke 14 languages.

Maurice was born in the Ural Mountains in Russia. He had French parents. Aged 17 he moved to France. In 1937 he became a wrestler, fighting in France and England. World War II meant he had to move to the USA in 1939.

He became a popular wrestler in the US, wrestling as The French Angel. In his 20s he developed acromegaly. Acromegaly is a condition caused by a benign tumor on the pituitary gland. This results in bone overgrowth - thickening of the bones. He passed away in 1954. But in 1980 he made a communication from the grave.

Patrick Kelly, an American businessman made contact with Maurice. He had been friends with Maurice when he was alive and they regularly played chess together. When they had played chess Maurice had often complained about his body and had often said:

"How awful it is to be imprisoned inside this body".

Later when they played chess Maurice said he was glad to be outside of his body and able to concentrate on the chess.

Kelly had a plaster death mask made of Tillet's face. He kept this at his desk. Also on his desk was an electronic chess set. He would often play against a computer opponent on this machine.

One evening Kelly was playing a game with the machine when Maurice made his first ghostly appearance. The computer chess program made a different move from the usual array of computerised moves. It used an 18th century chess game opening devised by a French chess player. It was one of Maurice's favourite openings. Kelly completed the game of chess and went to bed.

The next morning he made a rather strange discovery. The chess machine had not actually been plugged in. Several weeks later the machine tuned on and made the same opening again. Again it was not plugged in.

Kelly decide to get an engineer in to check the chess machine for faults. He wanted to see if it could work without being plugged in. The engineers made an odd discovery. The chess machine worked while not plugged in as long as Tillet's death mask was close to it. The mask was X-rayed to see if any special electrical device were inside. The check proved that no special electronic devices were inside the plaster death mask. It was solid plaster.

Kelly said that afterwards he would start a game

with the machine unplugged to see if the Tillet
would play. Also when playing the computer with
the machine turned on sometimes it would
suddenly perform at a higher standard half way
through the game - notifying Kelly that his old
friend was playing another game from beyond the
grave.

Brazilian Fire Balls

On the 17th June 1970 Maria Machado looked out
of thw window at her house in Rio De Janerio,
Brazil. She had just been preparing lunch. She
looked up into the sky and saw a strange metallic
disc floating towards the sea. The disc seemed to
have a "transparent dome". Maria thought she
spotted several people in silver suits moving
around the deck of the craft.

The craft slimmed the surface of the sea and then
took off and disappeared about an hour after she
first spotted it. The craft was also seen by Maria's
husband, 4 daughters. A policeman in the locality
also reported sighting the mysterious object.

On September 12th 1971 Paulo Silveira claimed
that two figures clad in blue boiler suits drugged
him and forced him into a strange disc type craft.
Silveira, a typewriter mechanic, had been driving
north of Rio when he saw a flying disc blocking
the road. A beam of light came from the craft
which had the effect of drugging Paulo.

Later he vaguely remembered two aliens "about the size of 10 year old children carried him aboard their spaceship. He did not recall anything that happened to him on the craft. He remembers only being carried out again and placed in his car. it was there he was found later by a motorist. He was taken to hospital. He could not recall what happened for three hours upon the craft.

A farmer Domingo Brito, also claimed to see a similar craft some 10 years later in January 1971. A grey saucer landed in his farm. Two "human like" aliens emerged and asked the farmer various questions in Portuguese. The craft then took off, The farmer could not recall the questions, and even though the aliens said they would return, they never did.

In 1980 a strange incident happened in the town of Tres Coroas south of Rio. For a period of 20 days fire shapes terrorized the city, chasing cars and roaming the city without igniting anything. Jose de Nacrento had a bicycle shop in the city. One evening he was going home when a fiery object followed his car. He managed to get home. He later said he though the fire was "after him". At home his son Vicente also reported seeing strange events. He saw an onion shaped UFO in the sky rotating and changing colour from orange to blue to green.

A local estate agent also reported seeing the craft and its shadow in the town. He reported that the saucer was moving rapidly. Two other saucers were also spotted, causing the estate agent to crash his car into another.

Local military police officer Antonio dos Gacas Santos saw his neigbour's garden lit up by s mysterious light. He rushed over to see what was happening and saw a human like figure standing in the garden with outstretched arms. His neighbour approached the strange creature and touched it. He received a shock. Suddenly everything went dark and the saucers disappeared.

Ghost Swimmers

On December 2nd 1929 sailors James Courtney and Michael Meehan were buried at sea. They worked on an oil tanker called the Watertown The tanker was owned by the cities Services Corporation and bound from California to Panama. Courtney and Meehan were killed by fumes while working below deck. They were asphyxiated.

The two sailors were popular, One crewmate was quoted as saying "they made everyone feel good".

After the burial at sea strange incidents started to occur on the voyage. One day after the burial the crew were surprised to see two men swimming near the ship. the ship slowed and prepared to rescue the men. But as they drew closer the swimmer seemed to fade away. The crew realised that the swimmers must be their late crewmates Courtney and Meehan.

For the next three days the two swimmers swam near to the ship. The crew were not alarmed as they knew their former crewmates did net pose a threat. At one stage it seemed as if the swimmers were trying to warn the crew about a weather event and divert the ship.

Later the captain of the ship Captain Tracy was in the New Orlean's office of the owners of the ship. Tracy told them about ghostly swimmers and they were the former crew members. The ship's owners gave Captain Tracy a camera and asked him to take photos of the supernatural swimmers on the next voyage.

On the Watertown's next journey they again saw the swimmers in the Pacific. The Captain duly took a number of photos before the swimmers vanished into thin air after a few hours of swimming near the ship.

When the ship returned to port, Captain took the film to the photographer to be developed. The shipping company executive monitored the process.

Most of the negatives did not come out properly. But finally the two swimmers were seen on one of the negatives.

Prints were made. Friends and relatives looked at the photos and identified the swimmers as James Courtney and Michael Meehan.

Soon the crew of the Waterton changed and the two swimmers no longer made their appearances.

Beitbridge Saucer

In 1974 Peter and his wife Frances were driving from Salisbury in Rhodesia (now Harare, Zimbabwe) on an overnight trip to Durban in South Africa. The road was empty.

Between Umvuma and Beitbridge they saw some very strange lights in the sky. Suddenly it felt as if their car had been taken over by a strange force. The car seemed to be floating over the road. The landscape looked unreal - almost dreamlike.

Peter fell into a dreamlike state and completely lost track of time. Frances later said she had slept through the whole incident.

Later on they saw that the car had much less petrol than it should of for the period of the journey. They then realised that a period of time had passed that they could not recall.

Peter had some experience of the paranormal previously in his life. Aged 13 he had been with his father on a long delivery run delivering various electrical goods. On the way, outside the town of Shabani, they spotted a UFO. Later when unloading the electronics they found that the circuits in the equipment had been destroyed by a power surge. Had the surge come from the UFO?

Around the time he saw the UFO in 1974 Peter also had an out of body experience and "dreams of floating".

Peter was hypnotized to see if he could remember anything about his encounter with the UFO. He remembered an alien "beaming down" to his car. The alien had used telepathic powers to show Peter a glimpse of their spacecraft. On it was a lab in which they experimented on humans.

One bizarre thing the aliens told Peter was they adapted a form which the human liked. The form most popular and the one they adopted for Peter was a small hairless human with no reproductive organs".

The aliens said there were many of them living as humans - thousands even. They tried to influence humans to get them to stop activities such as war. They never intervened directly by showing their true form or attacking military bases.

Peter was vague a to where the aliens came from. They stated that they were from the future or from "outer galaxies".

Phantom Houses

One April evening in 1955 Mrs Susannah Stone was driving home from a dinner with a friend. She was driving just outside the town of Ross and Cromerty in the north of Scotland. It was 9.30 in the evening. Mrs Stone and her friend were surprised to see a house on fire.

The house looked like a farmhouse. Mrs Stone said the house looked like it was about a quarter of mile/400m away. She and her friend decided to have a closer look. But as they got closer to the blazing house they received a shock: the house was not actually there.

Mrs Stone dropped her friend off home. She was still curious about the incident and the mystery of the phantom burning house so decided to return to the site of the fire. She found no evidence of the house, or any fire. There was not any rubble, ashes or anything else which signifying a house fire.

Upon further research she found that no house had even been on the site of the phantom fire. There had been another fire in the area which the fire brigade had been called out to on the same evening. This was to attend to a fire at a haystack.

Could this have been the fire that Mrs Stone saw? Had she confused the burning haystack with a burning house?

Maybe not as the haystack was some 30 miles away from the site of the phantom burning house - and in the opposite direction.

In 1955 Mr and Mrs Fraser were driving to Herstmonceux in Sussex, England. They were going to enjoy a pleasant weekend in country. They were driving from London.

About two hours out of London they spotted a rather delightful hotel. It looked like a traditional old English country house. The walls were covered in Lichen and there was a gravel drive. An extension with a sloping roof had been built. There was a neon sign with "American Bar" written on it.

The couple were booked into another local hotel. But, as this hotel looked so inviting they decided to return after their dinner at the other hotel for a few drinks.

Unfortunately when they returned to the site of the hotel they could not find it. It had just disappeared. The Frasers were very confused and slightly angry that they could not find the hotel they had almost certainly seen that evening.

Years afterwards when they drove along this road to visit relatives in the south of England they always searched for the hotel. They never managed to locate it again.

Alien Space Wreckage

In 1979 a strange claim was made by Soviet Union scientists. They claimed that an alien spaceship was orbiting the Earth.

The spaceship had – according to the scientists - been damaged. Another even more outlandish suggestion was that the craft contained the bodies of alien beings.

Professor Sergei Boshich said that the spaceship wreckage had first been spotted in the 1960s when it was some 1250 miles from Earth. It consisted of about ten pieces of wreckage. Some pieces were 30 metres/100 feet across.

They put the data concerning the wreckage into a computer. They wanted to try and trace the age of the wreckage. The pieces of wreckage were found to have originated in the same area. The date of the wreckage's accident was pinpointed at December 18th 1955 - two years before the first human spacecraft in 1957.

Soviet astrophysics expert Professor Aleksander Kazantsev said the wreckage pointed to the size of the craft: 60 metres/200 feet long and 30 metres/100feet wide. It had several floors, porthles and various rooms. Kazantsev stated:

"we believe alien bodies will be on board".

Meteors were ruled out as a possibility the object. They do not have an orbit or suddenly explode. Dr Vladimir Azhazha thought the craft would have "secrets we have not even dreamed of". Americans wee interested in the news. Dr Henry Monteith a physicist working in New Mexico said the wreckage should be looked in to:

"we should send up a pace shuttle. If it is an alien spacecraft it would be the find of the century".

Nuclear physicist and legendary UFO researcher Stanton Friedman suggested that if all the pieces of the craft were retrieved, the craft could be put back together.

The mystery of the space ship was never resolved. Or maybe the craft and the alien bodies was retrieved in secret and is hiding in a facility such as Area 51. Conspiracies about wreckage of alien space craft abound - one famous one being the Black Knight alien satellite. This theory claims an alien spacecraft is orbiting Earth and its existence is covered up by authorities.

Bob Taylor

Bob Taylor - a forester - worked for the Development Corporation of Livingston, East Lothian, Scotland. In 1979 he had an extremely bizarre encounter in a local wood.

On November 9th he was walking his dog up Dechmont Hill. He smelt a strong charcoal smell. Curious, he went to find out what was causing the smell. He walked to a clearing and was shocked to see two flying craft that looked like space vehicles. Two strange objects emerged looking like "wheels with arms".

The strange things started to claw at Taylor's legs, scratching them. He passed out during the ordeal; he woke 20 minutes later. Later when he came too, the weird objects and spacecraft had disappeared.

He managed to get home. Taylor's wife Mary called the police as Bob was "in such a state". they checked the clearing, and found Taylor's van: the engine was still running. Police found marks in the clearing. Policeman Ian Wark said:

"There were about 32 holes, which were about 3.5 inches in diameter, as well as marks similar to those made by the type of caterpillar tracks often fitted on bulldozers."

The marks did not go anywhere outside the clearing and police said:

"There appeared to be no rational explanation for these marks."

There were also heel marks in the clearing which showed that Taylor had been dragged.

Taylor's boss Malcolm Drummond looked at the area and the lack of marks leading to the clearing was puzzling. Drummond said that Taylor was not the sort of person who would make up a story about being attacked by alien creatures. Taylor was a teetotaler, war hero and a churchgoer and respected in the community.

On the same day Taylor had his experience a local woman also saw strange things in the sky. 72 year old Mary Hume of Easterhouse, Glasgow saw a pale white ball in the sky. She saw it break up in two, before joining up again.

Bob died in 2007. The incident has been called "one of very few hardcore cases that defied any explanation." There is now a special UFO trail at the site of the incident giving more information about the event and where it occurred.

Matthew Manning

In 1971 young Englishman Matthew Manning had a strange experience when he met a 300 year old ghost.

Matthew lived in a 19th century house in the village of Linton, Cambridgeshire. One day he saw a strange figure on the staircase. At first he thought it was a burglar; but in fact it was a ghost. Matthew managed to sketch the ghost before it disappeared.

Matthew learned more about the ghost over the following weeks. He was born in 1678 and had been born in the house. The ghost had built the front part of the house in 1730. That was the part of the house the ghost liked to haunt. The ghost's name was Robert Webbe and had died in 1733.

The ghost wore clothes from the 1720s, including a wig. He was often seen wearing a green frock coat, cream cravat and frilled cuffs. The ghost complained often about having poorly legs and walked using two sticks. The ghost talked to Matthew, apologizing for causing him "much fright".

After Matthew's encounter with the ghost, he acquired a selection of paranormal powers. One such power was that of automatic writing - where a person's writing is influenced by another person or entity. Robert exchanged messages with the ghost learning facts about its life.

In July 1971 Webbe wrote a number of messages on the wall of Mathhew's bedroom in pencil, Matthew never saw anyone or anything actually writing the messages. The messages were written in different handwriting styles and were signed by Webbe, his family and other people who had lived in the area in the past. The people writing the messages had lived between 1355 and 1959.

Other members of Matthew's family saw some supernatural occurrences. Matthew's father Derek experienced some strange sensations while in bed. Rather bizarrely he felt "the scratching of a man's beard on the sheets" and that another body had been superimposed onto his. One other experience was of sitting on a cage looking at rocks with a purple sky. Another odd experience was of being in someone's mouth.

Derek also had the supernatural symptoms off gout with a tingling in the foot. Gout was probably the cause of the ghost's bad legs.

The ghost often moved objects such as paintings and antiques around the house. Beds would suddenly look like they had been slept in with indentations on the pillow. Rotten fish and mouldy books would be smelt. Footsteps were heard on the stairs and a bell was rang in the hallway.

The ghost admitted causing these things to happen as "it was his house and he could do whatever he wanted to whenever he wanted". The ghost was proud of the house so it kept coming back - as long as - Matthew thought - that there were people with "psychic energy" in the house to be able to see him.

After the ghostly encounter Matthew developed supernatural powers such as being able to bend spoons, stop clocks and "stop electricity". Matthew has been in the public eye for his work as a healer and for his psychic abilities writing books and helping people. He has invited discussion of his abilities by investigators into the paranormal who have been sceptical about his abilities and his ghost stories.

Heathrow Airport

Heathrow Airport in London is a busy place with many passengers on an average day. There are also a large number of ghostly visitors to the airport. These ghoulish characters do not travel anywhere but instead linger around the airport.

One ghost is said to "pant like a dog" creeping up behind stewardesses. It is said to be Dick Turpin. One of Britain's most notorious highwaymen Turpin (1705-1739) took part in a series of crimes such as horse and livestock theft, murder and robbery. A popular legend is that he only robbed rich people. He was executed for his crimes in 1739 and played up to his popularity by smiling and playing at the crowd at his hanging.

At the airport he is seen wearing a tri corned hat, which was worn in his time. An airline company employee reported hearing strange noises - almost as if the man making the noises was right next to them. Others reported hearing weird animal noises. there does not seem to be a natural explanation for the strange noises.

Another Heathrow ghost is seen wearing a light grey suit and as a result has been called The Ghost in the Light Grey Suit. Once an African

dignitary saw the ghost and promptly ran odd
frightened from an airport VIP lounge. The ghost
in the light grey suit is said to haunt a VIP suite at
Euro Terminal, which is usually used by
Ambassadors, Heads of State and Royalty. The
African diplomat reported seeing the bottom half
of a man wearing grey trousers". The grey suited
ghoul has been seen many times and sceptics
have no explanation for his presence.

Another ghost is one which haunts Runway 1. He
has been describes as 6 feet tall and wearing a
bowler hat. The ghost always seems to be longing
for something.

Some have speculated that it is linked to a plane
crash that occurred in 1948. On an extremely
foggy night a Belgian Airways DC3 Dakota plane
The crash killed 22 business passengers. No one
survived. Rescue workers reported being asked by
a bowler hatted man where his briefcase was.
Workers reported pulling the bowler hatted man's
body from the wreckage later on. He is still
spotted looking for something and looking
confused. It is speculated that he is searching for
his briefcase.

Hand of Glory

In the 1700s thieves had a strange superstition to
try and ensure success for their criminal
endeavours. A person they intended to rob could

be made to sleep by placing a candle in the severed hand of a person who had been hanged.

The ingredients of the candle were said to include fat from the hanged man. Or as the 1722 Petit Albert Book of Magic described the ingredients:

"...make a kind of candle from the fat of a gibbeted felon, virgin wax, sesame, and make a kind of candle from the fat of a gibbeted felon, virgin wax, sesame, and ponie".

It was called the Hand of Glory.

A strange story about thieves using this macabre thieving method was reported in County Durham, England in the 1790s. A traveller arrived at the Old Spital Inn near Barnard Castle, The traveller wore women's clothes and asked to rest by the log fire.

A maid at the inn was suspicious after she spotted that the woman was wearing trousers under her skirt. The traveller then jumped up after pretending to sleep. It was a man, and he had the severed hand of a hanged criminal. He put a lit candle in the hand. He went to open the door of the in to let in his fellow robbers. The maid jumped up and locked the door. The robbers outside tried to smash the door open. The maid ran upstairs to wake the landlord and the staff. But they were asleep and she could not rouse him. Had the Hand of Glory worked?

The maid remembered another part of the superstition. The spell could be broken by throwing milk over the lit candle to extinguish it. She got a jug of milk and tossed it over the severed hand holding the candle. The landlord and the staff woke up and the thieves had to flee - especially as the landlord was armed with a shotgun.

Carol Thomas

Carol Thomas 45 and her 24 year old daughter Helen both worked in a mill in Birmingham. Every morning Helen went to her mother's house and they walked together to work.

On the 30th March 1988 they were walking to work in the dark. They heard a strange humming sound. Then a large spotlight seemed to shine above their heads. The next thing the two felt was a dizzy and confused feeling as they were in an alleyway. when they reached work they saw that they were late. The could not recall what had happened after glimpsing the spotlight. Their skin was sore, similar to sunburn. They had suffered nosebleeds.

Carol Thomas had hypnosis treatment in order to try and recall what had happened between seeing the spotlight and appearing the alleyway. She stated that she remembered being in a white windowed room. She was naked and strapped down to a table. Aliens were in the room with her. They had large black eyes and hands with three fingers.

A different alien seemed to be in charge. He was tall with blonde hair and blue eyes. He wore a silver suit. His suit had a distinctive badge - a blue one consisting of a circle, a triangle and two wavy lines. They pushed a long tube into her body. Carol thought they were taking her eggs.

Carol recalled that she was shown a war film and a series of shapes. She was made to wear a cup on her head.

Helen was also hypnotised. She recalled being strapped to a table. She had a small ball implanted into her nose. Wires and tubes were inserted into her nose and ears. Helen recalled her mother wearing a silver suit. The atmosphere on the ship was "clammy" When they woke in the alleyway after the abduction they were damp. Their clothes were wet.

Helen's hypnotic therapy made her recall another abduction. When she was years old she was taken from a "field full of buttercups" and examined by odd looking children. The children gave her a mysterious stone which Helen kept in her bedroom.

Helen recalled other abductions in her life and seems she was a regular subject of alien visitors.

The Iranian Cafe

In the 1950s civil engineer Tony Clark was working in Iran. He was working on the building of a cement factory. He had to make a 150 mile drive from Manjil located near the Caspian Sea to the Iranian capital Tehran. In Manjil Clark and his Iranian travelling companion did not have much to eat. The town was quite remote. The two of them had to make do with a breakfast of simple bread and watery yogurt.

The men drove through the Iranian countryside with no access to a town where they thought they might find a decent meal. They thought that if they were lucky they would find a roadside cafe. But they were lucky: they found one.

The cafe was run by an Armenian called Mr Hovanessian. He spoke perfect English. The cafe was packed with Iranian lorry drivers. Tony Clark and his companion looked forward to a substantial meal. The meal was delicious. There was a yogurt, raisin and cucumber iced soup; stuffed vine leaves and kebab. Wonderful Turkish coffee rounded off the meal. Mr Hovanessian invited them to return to the cafe at any time. He presented them with a ridiculously small bill. The men noted down the mileage from Manjil to the cafe so they could call in again in the future.

Three months later Tony Clark was again making the journey from Manjil to Tehran. He had told a number of people about his sumptuous meal at the roadside restaurant and was travelling with an English colleague who doubted such as restaurant existed. They approached the spot where the restaurant had been. But it was not the same. There was no sign of Mr Hovanessian.

Clark asked villagers about the roadside cafe. "There has not been such a cafe here for 40 years" one of them told him. For years afterwards Clark was certain the restaurant was real and had served him the best meal he had ever had. It seems that it was a phantom restaurant - that may have exited in the past.

Eusapia Palladino

Eusapia Palladino was a 19th century medium based in Bari, Italy. Palladino was poorly educated and was an orphan for much of her life. Her father was killed by thieves; her mother died giving birth.

In 1866 Palladino travelled to Naples to work as a nursemaid. In London an Italian psychic investigator called Damiani attended seance. A spirit named John King told of a powerful medium living in Italy. King stated that the medium was his reincarnated daughter. King even gave the address of Palladino's workplace.

After being discovered as a medium Palladino

embarked on a series of seances and lectures. At her seances objects moved through the air as musical instruments played themselves. Palladino was able to elongate her body, growing some 5 inches/13 cm in height.

Psychic researchers were naturally interested in Palladino. She was invited to New York, Paris and London to hold seances. Sceptics could see no signs of fraud. Palladino even often had her hands strapped down to avoid fraud. But some such as the magician J.N. Maskey said she was using conjuring tricks to levitate the table and various other objects. Other investigators stated that it was obvious she was using magic and deception in her seances.

But Palladino had supporters among those who investigated psychic mediums. They said the fraud she committed at her show was because she could not conduct her seances properly on a particular evening and did not want to disappoint her audiences. They also said that much of her psychic work was unexplainable.

Holy Aubergines

In 1990 Farida Kassan was preparing dinner in her home in Leicester, England. She sliced open an aubergine (eggplant). But Farida and her husband Zahid were surprised to find an Islamic devotional message written in the seeds of the sliced vegetable. The message Yah-allah - God Exist was written.

The couple showed the sliced vegetable to a non-Muslim friend who also clearly saw the massage written in the seeds. After a few weeks the couple got permission from their mosque to make the discovery public. 5000 people visited them in one week to view the message. Eventually the aubergine started to rot away; it was buried on holy ground.

The Muslim community in the area was interested in the vegetable. The owner of the store where the aubergine was bought had many visitors because of the vegetable. Many bought aubergines hopping to find religious messages.

More spiritual messages were indeed found. One had a verse from the Koran. One spelled Allah. One man even got his scientist son to preserve a holy vegetable slice in saline solution.

Were there really holy messages in the vegetables? Or were the messages just similar to the normal seed patterns and found as people just wanted to see a spiritual message?

It has been suggested that this may have been part of a phenomena around the world at the time. In Algeria a cloud was seen which spelled the word Allah. In India a mango was found upon which was written the phrase La Ilaha Illahah - There Is no God But Allah.

Some have suggested the messages coincided with the Gulf War which saw Christian countries in the Middle East.

The sightings continued after 1990. In 1996 Ruksana Patel from Bolton, England saw the Yah-allah message again in an aubergine. Mrs Patel had had dreams that the aubergine she bough at the store would be blessed.

In 1998 Khadija Yakoob, 13 of Blackburn, England saw the Arabic for Allah is Everywhere written on an aubergine slice. She said:

"It is obvious we have been blessed, and to receive it at this time, during the month of Ramadan, is very special. They [her mosque] said it only came to lucky people who were entitled to paradise so it is quite an honour".

Willington Mill

In 1835 Joseph Proctor moved into the Willington Mill house with his family. The house was quite new and located in the village of Willington in Northumberland. It was beside a stream and very picturesque. They were not interested in local rumours that the house was haunted.

The family were very respected. They were Quakers and very kind to each other and everyone they met such as their employees. Soon they were driven mad by the ghostly occupants of the house.

The site of the house used to be the site of an old cottage. A horrible crime was committed at the cottage. A priest had refused to hear the confession of a woman who had lived there. Writer and ghost hunter W.T. Stead found more than forty people who had seen ghosts at Willington Mill.

In January 1835 a nursemaid was putting some children to sleep at the mill. The second floor had a nursery. Above the nursery was an empty room. suddenly the nurse heard footsteps coming from the empty room above. She though that workmen must be up there, but the noises and footsteps continued. They got increasingly louder. Members of the family living in the house and the staff also heard the noises. When someone opened the door to check the room no one was found.

On one morning Mr Proctor was with his family when footsteps were heard on the stairs. They continued into the hall and on to the front door. Bolts and locks were heard unlocking. Mr Proctor went to investigate. No one was there, but footsteps were heard on the path and in the garden.

The servants increasingly left the mill because of the supernatural incidents. One young servant Mary Young had been with the Proctor family for a while and loyally stayed on.

The house seemed to be taken over by "unseen forces". hidden people would open doors, enter and leave the room, breath extremely loudly. The steps of a child and sounds of furniture being moved were heard.

One day the ghosts were finally seen. Mary Young was washing some dishes in the kitchen. She heard footsteps. She looked in the passageway and saw a woman in a lavender silk dress. The lady climbed the stairs then disappeared in to a room.

On another occasion two of Mrs Proctor's sisters arrived for a visit. They slept in a four poster bed. during the night they felt the bed lift up. They rang the alarm but no one was found in the room. Several times the bed was shaken and lifted up. One evening they had a ghoulish experience. A hazy blue figure of a lady came out of the wall and floated in front of them., before moving back into the wall.

One of the sisters decided to stay at the house of the foreman of the mill Thomas Mann and his family. One evening Thomas, his wife, daughter and one of the sisters went for a walk past the mill. They saw a ghostly figure of a priest on one of te windows gliding around the second floor, moving through the walls and looking out of the window. The haunting was in a room called the Blue Room.

Edward Drury a supernatural investigator was brought in to sleep in the room. Drury described his night. He said he saw a woman wearing greyish garments with her head down and her hand on her chest as if in pain. Drury had then fainted. After being taken out of the room it was some four hours before he was in a fit state to say what had happened. He said "for God's sake keep her off me".

Even though the Proctors did not want their children to see the ghosts eventually they did. The daughters reported seeing a lady "with no eyes" coming out of a wall. And a ghostly figure was seen pulling up some sash windows.

In 1847 the Proctors finally moved to another house in Northumberland. They had enough of the hauntings. Their home was split up into multiple dwellings and fell into disrepair. It was never haunted on the same scale after the Proctors left.

Spanish Red Lights

In 1979 a jet full of German and Austrian tourists took off from the Spanish holiday island of Majorca. The plane was piloted by Captain Francisco Javier Lerdo de Tejada - a 35 year old man who had been flying aircraft for 15 years.

The plane took off a 9.30 am bound for the

Canary Islands. Soon the pilot encountered something very strange in the sky. There were two very bright lights. The lights seemed to be flying in a set formation, and becoming increasingly closer to the plane. Soon they were about half a mile away.

The pilot radioed the control tower at Barcelona airport about the lights. They told him that there were no aircraft near his place: nothing was showing up on the radar.

The captain decided to call the Madrid radar station and the Spanish air force. The Madrid radar station had much better equipment and could pick up non-civilian air traffic more easily. The Madrid station had more success. Two objects were located flying close to the plane. The pilot decided to fly the plane upwards to try and escape the red lights. In response the red lights went down, and the Madrid station saw them drop 12000 feet (3.6 kn) in 31 seconds; another aircraft was not able to do this.

30 miles off the coast of Valencia the lights disappeared when a Spanish Mirage jet fighter appeared on the scene. The fighter tracked the object and called it a "truncated cone shape with a changing colour". Some of systems on the fighter jammed and went haywire before the object accelerated out of sight towards the coast of Africa.

The pilot took the plane to an airport in Valencia -

Manises. Captain Lerdo de Tejada filed a report of the strange incident. His story was backed up by the crew and the head of the Spanish Transport and Communication minister.

A Spanish government enquiry said the object may have been an optical illusion or caused by "flashes emitted from a distant chemical industry complex. The airline and fighter pilots on that day would beg to differ.

Robert Loosely

At 3.15 on the morning if October 4th 1871 carpenter Robert Loosely woke up at his house in High Wycombe, England. It was quite warm for an October night in England. Loosely decided to go for a walk in his garden to cool down.

In the garden he saw a strange light in the sky which looked like an extremely light star. The light was moving. He then heard a noise like a clap of thunder. Loosely thought this was rather odd as the sky was completely clear. The strange light then stopped and went straight down in the direction of some woodland. Robert went back to his house.

Later that day he decided to investigate the area where the light descended. There he discovered something metallic among some leaves. He found it was a metal container 20 metres/65 feet high.

To Loosely's surprise it opened and emitted a bright purple light. A small stick came out of the container. Loosely left the area but the object followed him, leaving a trail. He found this shape in another clearing in the wood. The object used the stick to collect a dead rat which it placed into the cylinder. Loosely wanted to get away but he found himself being herded by the object into a larger metal object. He saw more strange lights in the sky and managed to get home.

Later that night in his home he again saw strange lights in the area of the woodland where he had encountered the object. Eventually the lights went up into the sky and disappeared. He decided to write his strange experience down on a piece of paper. He locked the document in his desk.

One hundred years later Loosely's great great grandaughter discovered the document while clearing out her attic. An expert verified the authenticity of the document. Loosely died in 1893.

Royal Ghosts

Windsor Castle, the retreat of the British Royal Family is said to have at least 25 ghosts. It is said that four of them are former monarchs. Princess Margaret (Queen Elizabeth II's sister) said that she spotted Queen Elizabeth I walking around the castle. Queen Elizabeth I died in 1603. The ghost of Queen Elizabeth I seems to frequent the castle library most of all and has been spotted many times. Her heels are sometimes heard on the floorboards in the library. she is said to wear a black gown and black shawl.

Another famous ghost is that of Charles I. Charles was executed during the English Civil War in 1849. Charles has been seen numerous times in the library standing on a table.

George III died in 1820. He was insane and is often seen walking through the castle. He was put in the castle in his last years. His ghost is apparently heard to mutter "what what".

Henry VIII has been seen at the castle. In 1977 he was seen walking through a wall in the basement. There had been a door there during Henry's life. He has been heard often in the Cloisters of the castle groaning. He was killed by an ulcerated leg and this is said to be the source of his groans. Henry was buried at the castle in St George's Chapel.

In 1927 a guardsman killed himself at the castle. Soldiers on guard duty often spotted the ghost of the guardsman walking around the castle.

Richard II's forester Herne the Hunter is another who haunts Windsor Castle. Herne is seen wearing a deer skin and deer antler helmet. Many have spotted him with a pack of ghost hunting hounds. He was a keeper in the woods at Windsor Castle hired after he rescued the King from a stag attack. Herne was sacked from his job as keeper after being accused of poaching. It is speculated that he was framed by those who thought he was involved in black magic. After being sacked Herne hanged himself.

King Richard II saw the ghost of Herne in the forest. A bolt of lightening struck a tree and then Richard saw the figure of Herne with dear antlers on his head. Richard was not finding any deer in the forest. Those who framed Herne admitted what they had done and suggested that might be behind the lack of deer. Richard killed Herne's accusers and the deer returned. It is said that Herne's ghost told Richard II to execute the accusers.

In 1863 Queen Victoria cut down the tree Herne hanged himself from. She burnt the logs in her home fireplace to exorcise the ghost. But the sightings of Herne go on. In 1963 schoolboys from Eton school saw the ghost of Herne at the woods at Windsor. One of them found an old hunting horn on the grass. He blew it and it seemed to rouse the ghost of Herne who appeared with his men riding towards the children. The schoolboys ran off frightened. In 1976 a guardsman at the castle said that he had seen a strange thing happen in the Italian garden. One of the statues had come to life. It seemed to grow deer antlers in its head.

Ghosts also haunt Hampton Court. Henry VIII's

5th wife Catherine Howard haunts the palace. Catherine had her head chopped off by Henry in 1547. She has been seen running towards the door of the chapel screaming.

Jayne Seymour is another of Henry VIII's wives seen at the palace. Seymour who was Henry's 3rd wife has frequently been seen walking through the Queen's apartments. She is normally seen carrying silver in the Silver Stick Gallery on the anniversary of her son's birth in 1537.

Jane died a week after the birth of her son, who later became Edward VI. 10 years after Jane Seymour's death Edward became King aged 10. He was looked after a nurse called Mistress Sibell Penn.

Penn has also been seen at the castle haunting it. Penn die of smallpox and in 1568 was buried at St Mary's Church, Hampton, London. in 1829 Penn's tomb was moved. Around the time the tomb was moved strange noises started to come from behind a wall at Hampton Court. The wall was subsequently knocked down revealing a hidden room. This room where Penn had lived.

After the tomb was moved Mistress Penn was often seen haunting Hampton court around the area where the room was. Penn has been described as a tall hooded figure wearing a grey robe and walking with her arms outstretched.

Balmoral in Scotland is also haunted. John Brown

assistant of Queen Victoria has been sighted walking around the corridors wearing a kilt. Even Queen Elizabeth II has reported seeing the ghost of Mr Brown.

Sandringham has a mysterious Christmas visitor in the guise of a poltergeist. It appears every year in the servant's quarters moving sheets and various objects through the air.

The ghost of Major John Gwynne haunts Buckingham Palace. Gwynne was a secretary in King Edward VIII's household. He was involved in a divorce case and thought the affair would tarnish the reputation of the Royal Family. So he shot himself in his office at Buckingham Palace. His ghost haunts the area where his office was located.

Kensington Palace has a number of ghostly visitors. In the courtyard a ghost wearing buckskin breeches is seen. An apparition of Princess Sophia, an aunt of Queen Victoria, is seen sitting in the palace working on a spinning wheel - she was a talented seamstress.

Another apparition is that of King George II who can be seen sitting on the roof of Kensington Palace sitting near a weather vane saying "why don't they care?". This somewhat odd remark is due to the fact that he was waiting for an important message via an aide from Hanover when he died in 1760.

The newest royals are also haunted. Prince Louis's nursery at the palace is haunted by a ghost called Peter the Wild Boy. During the reign of King George II (1727-1760) a man named Peter was seen in the hallways. He had Pitt Hopkins disease which caused his face to become deformed. He died in the palace.

Glamis Castle Monster

Glamis Catle in Angus in Scotland was said to have a rather strange creature - known as the Mad Earl.

There is thought to be a man shaped like an egg with thin legs and arms. The creature is said to be strong and hairy. It is said the creature was hidden from public view by the Strathmore Clan. The clan decided to lock the monster in a secret room at the castle.

Guests at the castle spoke of strange happenings at the castle. A woman reported spotting a strange white face staring at her from a window. Strange screams and noises were reported. In 1859 a guest at the castle named Mrs Munro saw a shape in her room and felt "a beard brush her face". The strange shape then moved into a room where her son was. Her son started to scream, there was a huge crash heard by Mr and Mrs Munro and their sons. Next morning at breakfast other guests said that they also heard a crash.

In 1865 a man working at the castle found a secret passage and saw a strange creature in the passage. The castle authorities gave him a large payment and helped him to emigrate.

In 1872 Augustus Hare, an author, attended a party at the castle. He reported that the Earl of Strathmore was looking particularly sad. The Bishop of Brechin asked if he could help. Lord Strathmore replied that he was in a very unfortunate position and that no one could help him.

Andrew Ralston was the land agent at the castle between 1860-1912. He asked Queen Elizabeth II's grandmother Countess Strathmore for the full story about the creature. Ralston said:

"It is very fortunate you do not know it - it would make you very unhappy".

The Queen Mother's sister Dowager Countess Granville once stated:

"our parents forbade us to discuss the monster or ask any questions about it."

The Queens's great grandfather, the 12th Earl said: if only you could guess the nature of the secret you would go down on your knees and thank god it was not you".

Ghost hunters have searched for clues about the

secret, looking at the family tree for clues of what the creature could be. One researcher said that Lord Glamis had a son called Thomas who was born and died on October 21 1825. It was posited that his son did not die, but was deformed. He was not expected to live long but had a long life and was cared for at the castle.

Galilee Glass

In the 1950s it was decided to build a museum in a cave near Haifa in Israel. The cave was the site of Beth She'arim, an ancient Jewish city which included graves in it's catacombs. The cave was silted up and entrance needed bulldozing.

After it was bulldozed a large slab was found. The slab was used as the base for a large model in the museum. This slab was in reality a very important archaeological find. Later local archaeologists examined the slab. They found it was not made of rock but of glass. The colour of the glass was purple and green. The glass slab was measured and found to be 3.4 x 1.64 metres (11.15 x 5.24 feet)) 50cm (1.64 feet) thick and weighed 9 tones. It was the third largest piece of glass ever discovered.

The first two largest pieces of glass were man made and were mirrors for telescopes made in 1934. This piece of glass was over a thousand years old. It was termed as the Great Glass Slab of Galilee.

In 1964 American experts led by Dr Robert Brill of the Corning Museum of Glass in New York investigated the glass slab. He was confused as to who had made the glass slab and why it was in Galilee. To make the glass would have required a complex process. Brill guessed that it had been created using a large furnace. Beneath the slab were huge stones which had been covered with clay which pointed to a large furnace. But why was the slab still there? Had the process gone wrong? Or maybe it had been a decorative piece that was not used.

Brill said it was a mystery that between the 4th and 7th centuries such a huge process was undertaken. He said:

"They brought over 11 tones of raw materials to a temperature of 100C for several days and created a glass consolidated mass. This was a considerable technological feat. I know of no similar accomplishment in the metallurgical or other pyrotechnic arts in ancient times."

Philip Spencer

On the first day of December in 1987 Philip Spencer was walking across IIkley Moor in Yorkshire. He was visiting his father in law who lived on the other side of the moor in a small village.

Spencer had left early in the morning around 7 am for the 5 mile journey. He had set off from IIkey town centre. Spencer had a compass.

He was walking near a quarry when he heard some strange noises. They were humming sounds - like a small aircraft. Then a very strange incident occurred. According to Spencer a small creature approached him. It was green in colour. Spencer threw a stone at the creature to try and scare it off. It worked as the creature moved away.

Spencer had taken a camera with him to take some pictures of IIkley town from the moor. He took a photo of the creature as it scuttled away. Spencer then discovered the creature's craft. It was a huge silver UFO which looked like two crafts welded together. The craft made a humming noise: similar to the one Spencer had heard earlier. The noise got increasingly louder, then the craft flew off vertically at a very high speed and disappeared into the sky.

Philip Spencer returned back to IIkley shocked by his strange experience. When he returned to the town it was rather busy which surprised him as he had left very early and it should have been about 8 am. But he was surprised to learn that it was 10 am. Philip remembered the photo he had taken of the bizarre green creature he had encountered on the moor. He went to Keighley and got the film developed as that town had a 1 hour photo developing service. He looked at the photos and found that the picture of the creature had been developed. It was slightly blurry, but the alien creature could be seen!

Spencer was in two minds whether to go public with the discovery as he was concerned that people would call him a crank. Indeed "Philip Spencer" is an alias as the individual in this tale did not want his real name known. He wanted to join the police force and though his talk of encountering aliens might jeopardize his career chances. Also he did not want to be seen as a hoaxer.

Instead he decided to take the matter to the Manchester UFO Research association. He contacted them using a PO Box number as his address. After a period he met the researchers of the group face to face. He gave them the photo and negatives so they could test them to see if they were real and had not been tampered with. Kodak labs said it was authentic. Many other experts have examined the photo since the incident and stated that it among other things it does not look like the alien has been superimposed on the image.

The UFO researchers - Jenny Randles and Peter Hough - concluded that the photo and negatives were real. Another discovery Spencer made was that the polarity of his compass had been reversed and rendered useless after his encounter with the alien. For the polarity to have been reversed it had to have been exposed to some sort of magnetic field - a dangerous and complex process.

Several weeks after the incident wit the alien, Spencer was visited by a Ministry of Defence team (or Men in Black!) who wanted to take the photo and negatives off him. Spencer told them that the UFO research group had them

Spencer decided to undergo hypnotic regression therapy. He had had strange dreams about floating lost in a starry sky. Maybe it had a connection with the two hours he lost on the moor.

During the hypnosis sessions he remembered being abducted by the aliens. He was paralysed by the creatures and then he floated up over the quarry and into the UFO. He was unconscious for a period. When he awoke he was in a brightly lit room. The aliens put him on an operating table and shone a light over him. They assured him that he was not being harmed. Something was stuck up his nose.

After the medical experiments Spencer was given a guided tour of the spaceship. He looked out of the window and saw the earth. The aliens showed him a number of films, including one with apocalyptic images. Later he woke up on the moor. The missing two hours had been spent on the alien spaceship.

When hypnotised he was able to give a better description of the aliens. They were 4 ft (1.2 meters) tall. They had pointy ears. The aliens had not tried to prevent him from taking the photo. Philip Spencer had no reason to make up such a strange story.

With good character references he was able to join the police. The sighting as gone down as one of the best pieces of evidence that extra terrestrials have visited Britain. Sceptics have suggested that the picture is rather grainy and could have been easy to fake using "a cardboard cutout".

Ghost Photos

In July 1964 Gordon Carroll, who worked in the office of a shoe factory in Northampton, England went on a holiday in his local area. He looked around the historic villages in his area.

He took photos of the old architecture and visited the village of Woodford to take some photos of the St Mary's Church. He took photos of the altar, the east window and the choir section. Several weeks later he looked at a the slides of the photos taken in the church. He was surprised to notice a transparent figure on the altar steps. The figure was kneeling.

When Gordon had taken the photos in the church

it had been completely empty. He wondered if the "ghostly figure" was a trick of the light in the photo. It was not as a result of a double exposure as Gordon's rather expensive camera prevented double exposures. It could have been caused by a reflection from the window; but because of the time Gordon took the photo this would not have been possible. Could it have been an apparition: a ghost?

The photo was taken to a forensic photo specialist. Their explanation was that the ghost was a cleaning lady brushing the steps. The photo had taken a long time to expose and was made up of a series of images of the cleaning lady. Gordon said that this could not be the case as he was certain that he was the only person in the church: he was adamant that there was no cleaning lady.

A newspaper article of the incident which include Gordon's photo is displayed in the church to this day.

On January 22nd 1985 the Coventry Freemen Association held a dinner event at St Mary's Guildhall in Coventry, England.

The photographer decided to have a longer than usual exposure as the room was rather dark when taking a picture of the diners at prayer.

Later when the photo was developed a strange robes figure was seen. The figure looked like a monk. The monk like figure was bowed and looked like it was praying as well.

No other person attending the event remembers someone looking like or dressed up as a Monk. Was it a ghost taking part in the prayers? Was it a trick of the light, or a result of the long exposure?

St Mary's Guildhall has a reputation for ghosts. As well as the monk who has been seen a his presence felt on other occasions there are other ghosts. These include a grey lady, a man in a skull cap, people dressed in Elizabethan attire and a small girl. Blood patches have appeared on the floor of the building. Growling noises are sometimes heard. Some visitors to the guildhall have felt a great feeling of sadness in certain rooms.

The Phantom London Bus

In June 1934 an accident occurred with a London bus. A car was driving to an intersection near Ladbroke Grove and Cambridge Gardens.

The street was rather empty. Suddenly at 1.15 am a red double decker bus numbered 7 appeared out of nowhere on the street. It charged at the car. The man driving the car was naturally shocked and in avoiding the bus crashed his car into a building. The car burst into flames. The driver survived with serious burns. He managed to tell the police what had happened before he sadly died of his injuries.

There were some eyewitnesses who confirmed
that the red double decker bus came out of
nowhere and drove into the unfortunate driver.
According to the eyewitnesses there were two
chilling factors in the crash. The bus had no one
on board (the bus was lit up so people could see
no one on board) and disappeared after the
accident.

Eyewitnesses said the bus had a number 7, and
was a London General bus with the word General
on the side. London General and gone bust one
year before the accident in 1933. London
Transport took over the route.

More sightings of this ghoulish bus were reported.
All the sightings were on St. Mark's Road. Some
have suggested it has carried on charging at cars
causing accidents. The Number 7 always appears
at 1.15 am. Some have tried to board the bus -
but the bus just disappears if this happens. There
is legend that if someone does board the bus then
they disappear forever. The bus is not interested
in pedestrians - just cars.

The sightings of the bus seemed to end in 1990
after the road and area was changed and
upgraded. One theory is the ghostly bus driver
was angry at how dangerous the intersection was,
and once it was made safer his phantom reign of
terror via bus came to an end.

Cheltenham Hauntings

Between 1882-1889 a series of hauntings occurred at a home in Cheltenham, England. At St Anne's house on Pittville Circus Road a woman in black appeared. She was tall and held a handkerchief on her face.

About twenty people reported seeing the ghost; twenty others said that they had heard the ghost. The residents in the house were Captain and Mrs Despard and their six children. Also present were their servants. The ghost was seen at all times of the day - including in the daylight. It is said that those who saw the apparition said that she looked like a "real physical person".

Despard's daughter Rosina described her:

"The figure was that of a tall lady, dressed in black of a soft woollen material, judging from the slight sound in moving. The face was hidden in a handkerchief held in the right hand Her left hand was nearly hidden by her sleeve and a fold of her dress. As she held it down a portion of a widow's cuff was visible on both wrists"

Thread was placed in the house to check if the ghost was a hoax. But the ghost passed through the thread. some have suggested that the ghost could have have been a hoax as those who saw the ghost were the Despard family, their servants and friends. No outsiders saw the ghost.

Rosina Despard was shown several photos of the women who had lived in the house. She was able to identify the "woman in black" as a wife of a previous owner. She was called Imagen Swinhole.

One person not associated with the Despard household saw the ghost fifty years after the Despard sightings. Later in the 20h century the house was turning into a boys boarding school. Some at the school reported seeing a ghostly lady in various parts of he house such as the corridors, gardens and stairs.

David McConnel

On 7th December 1918 18 year old David McConnel crashed his plane at Tadcaster in England and died. There was heavy fog and he had crashed nose first into the ground. His watch stopped at the moment of impact of the crash. The watch stopped at 3.25 pm.

A Royal Air force officer at David's funeral told him that a friend of David's that his ghost had been seen. McConnel shared a room with Lieutenant J.J. Larkin.

Between 3.15 am and 3.30 pm Larkin was sitting their room, 65 miles away from the scene of the crash. He thought he heard McConnel enter the room. McConnel would make lots of noise entering the room and would invariably shout the greeting "hello boy!". This is what Larkin heard. He saw McConnel standing in the doorway. McConnle was wearing his flying outfit. Strangely for a pilot he was wearing a naval cap. McConnel said "cheerio" then slammed the door and left.

Later an officer asked Larkin if McConnel had returned from his flight. Larkin said yes - as he though he had seen the real McConnel earlier. Later than evening Larkin heard about the accident which killed McConnel. He had seen him after his death: he had told the officer he had done so in the afternoon.

Skulls of the Lake District

Myles Phillipson owned a large portion of land in the English Lake District. during the 1500s. His land was next to Lake Windermere. He wanted more land and wealth and was always on the look out for more of them.

Krasner and Dorothy Cook owned a farm next to his land. It included a perfect spot which overlooked the picturesque Lake Windermere. Phillipson though this would be the ideal point to build a mansion for himself. The Cooks did not wish to sell their farm and turned down Phillipson's offers. They were very happy with their plot of land.

Phillipson decided to persuade the Cooks to sell by inviting them round to his house for a sumptuous Christmas dinner. Luxury foods and fine wines were served. The Cooks liked a golden bowl at the house and Phillipson said they could have it.

The next morning the Cooks were visited by soldiers. They were then taken to prison. They were not sure why they had been arrested until they were informed of their crime: stealing the golden bowl. The Cooks were put on trial. The man conducting the trial was the local magistrate: Myles Phillipson. He sentenced them to death. After the sentence Dorothy Cook said:

"You will never prosper...the time will come when you will own no land. You'll never be rid of us."

Soon after the Cooks were hanged Phillpson had acquired their land. He started construction of his large new home. The name of the new home was Calgarth Hall.

He finished it by the following Christmas after his crooked Christmas meal with the Cooks. He held an expensive Christmas party with friends and neighbours. Suddenly a huge scream was heard upstairs. People ran upstairs with their swords drawn to see what the commotion was. Phillipson made a gruesome discovery. On the bannister were two grinning skulls. Phillipson threw then into the courtyard on his new expensive home. He vowed revenge against whoever had placed the skulls in his house. But Phillipson had a problem:

the skulls kept returning to his house. Everytime he got rid of them they simply turned up again.

News of the Phillipson haunting spread around the area. His business was ruined and his money dribbled away.

When he died his home was filled with the laughter of the demonic skulls. The skulls hunted Phillipson's heirs haunting the house. Each Christmas and on the anniversary of the Cooks hanging they made a special grisly appearance.

Eventually Phillipson's heirs could not afford the mansion. Only then did the gruesome supernatural skulls end their haunting of Calgarth Hall.

Ghost Cyclist

It was a cold winter night in a small village near Northampton. It was 1940 and Britain was at war with Germany. It was a particularly cold winter with snow and frost everywhere. George decided to go to his local pub The Fox and Hounds to have a beer and some entertainment.

George walked over to the pub. As he was passing the cemetery and car came towards him. He could just make out the headlights. Next to the car was a cyclist which he was just able to make out in the icy fog and snow. The cyclist looked to be struggling to control his cycle in the ice.

George then made a ghoulish discovery: the cyclist had no head. He considered that he may be seeing things and that it could have been a trick of the light. The light was rather strange after all because of the wintry weather conditions. Also the cyclist may have been wearing a hat and thick scarf so his face may have been obscured.

The car carried on and looked to have hit the cyclist: it drove through the cyclists 's path. George looked for the cyclist to see if it had been hurt in an accident. But the cyclist was nowhere to be seen. He again searched for the cyclist but could not find anything.

George went to the pub. He was shaken and told the people about his experience. When he had finished recounting his tale Lid Green the local gravedigger finished his glass of beer then said:

"That sounds like the chap I buried 25 years ago. He was knocked off his bike in some snow outside the cemetery gates. His head was taken off in the crash".